Contents

Written by
Benjamin Hulme-Cross

Illustrated by
Daniel Tarrant

T0345662

Series editor **Dee Reid**

ALWAYS LEARNING

PEARSON

Luke

Donna

Joe

Aunty Annie

New vocabulary

ch1 p3 clanged

ch1 p4 recently

ch3 p14 squealed

ch3 p14 grimly

ch4 p16 disguise

ch4 p20 solved

Introduction

My name is Joe and Luke is my best friend. Luke thinks he's so smart at working things out. He really fancies himself as a detective. One day a girl called Donna asked us to help her aunty. We went up to her aunty's flat and a few strange things had been going on. Can Luke use his detective skills to solve the case?

The Locked Room

Chapter One

Luke fancies himself as a detective. He thinks he's so smart at working out problems. One day, we were having a kick around when a girl called Donna ran out of the flats. Something clanged on the ground. Donna picked it up and then ran over. "You've got to help me," she gasped. "I think my aunty is in trouble."

"What's happened?" Luke asked.

"I saw a guy dressed in black running out of her flat. Please come!" said Donna.

There had been loads of doorstep muggings in the area recently. We ran with Donna up to the flat. The front door was wide open. Outside the door was a red sports bag.

"Whose bag is that?" Luke asked.

"It's mine," said Donna.

We went inside the flat.

"Aunty Annie?" Donna called. There was no answer. We checked all the rooms.

"This room is locked," said Luke. He bent down and looked through the key hole. Then he told Donna and me to look too.

On the floor was the body of a woman. She wasn't moving. Just then a phone buzzed. Donna snatched it out of her pocket and switched it off.

"OK, we'll have to break in," said Luke.

This was my chance to show off my kung fu skills.

I planted a kick in the middle of the door. The door flew open and we burst into the room.

Chapter Two

Aunty Annie groaned and sat up. "Who are you?" she croaked.

"It's OK Aunty Annie, these boys are here to help," said Donna looking pale. "What happened?"

"I don't know," began Aunty Annie. She rubbed the side of her head.

"That's a big bruise you've got there," said Luke.

"I was about to call the bank when the doorbell rang," explained Annie. "I had my mobile in my hand when I went to the door. There was a short guy dressed in black. He had a scarf over his mouth so I couldn't see his face. He must have hit me, dragged me into this room and taken my mobile."

I was looking at the door I'd kicked in. I was feeling quite proud of myself. That was why I noticed the key.

"This door was locked with a key," I said.

"So?" said Luke.

I pointed at the lock. "The key is still in the lock. The door was locked from the inside!"

Chapter Three

"Have a look around and see if anything else has been stolen," Luke said to Annie.

Annie began to look around her flat.

"Either she's a bit loopy," I said, "or she's just making it up."

Donna nodded. "You're right. There's no way someone else could have locked the door. She must be going round the bend." "How dare you talk like that when I do so much to help you and your Mum!" snapped Annie as she came back into the room. "Who do you come to when you're short of money?"

Then she turned to Luke, "Nothing else has been taken," she told him.

"Why would someone take just your phone?" Luke asked.

Annie gave a cry. "Oh no! It's got all my bank passwords saved on it! Quick, I should call the bank so no one can get into my savings! I need someone's phone."

I reached for my phone but Luke stopped me.

"Donna," he said. "Could Annie borrow your phone?"

"OK," said Donna, looking nervous. She handed a mobile to Annie.

"How do I look up the bank's phone number on your phone?" asked Annie.

"Wait," said Luke. "I think Donna knows where your phone is."

"What? You're crazy," snapped Donna.

"Then you won't mind emptying your pockets," said Luke.

"No way. What... Ow!" Donna squealed as Annie caught her arm.

"It wouldn't be the first time she's stolen from me," Annie said grimly. "Hold her still while I check her pockets."

I did as I was told. A couple of seconds later, Annie was waving another phone under Donna's nose. "You little rat!" she hissed. "I know you've nicked the odd tenner before. But knocking me out? You've gone too far."

Chapter Four

Donna started crying. "I'm really sorry Aunty Annie. I never meant to hurt you. I just pushed the front door too hard and it hit your head."

"But you still planned to get at my savings didn't you?" Annie spat. "You came here in disguise! Get out! GET OUT!" Donna ran.

"Will you call the police?" asked Luke.

"I don't know," Annie sounded sad.

"She's family so I'll talk to her mum first. They don't have much but I can't believe she went this far!" She paused, then looked puzzled.

"I have to ask, how did you guess it was Donna?"

"All the clues were there," said Luke
importantly. "The phone she gave you
to call the bank was purple. But the one
I saw her switch off earlier was silver." He
pointed at the silver phone in Annie's hand.
"And it had to be someone who knew you
kept your passwords on your phone."

"But it was a guy wearing black," Annie said.

"You never saw his face though," replied
Luke, "and I bet that red sports bag has a
set of black clothes in it."

"So why did she get you guys involved?" asked Annie.

"My guess is she felt really bad when she saw she'd knocked you out and wanted to check you were OK," said Luke.

"What about the locked door?" I asked.

"Simple!" said Luke. "Donna must have run out of the flat with the key by mistake. We heard her drop something when we were outside."

"Donna must have put the key into the lock after we had looked through the keyhole," explained Luke. "If she had just thrown the key away she might have got away with it."

So Luke had solved the mystery of the locked room... but he couldn't have done it without my kung fu skills!

Quiz

Literal comprehension
p9 What does Joe notice about the lock on the door?
p12 Why did Donna want Aunty Annie's phone?
p18–19 How had Luke worked out that the criminal was Donna?

Inferential comprehension
p11 Why does Donna want the boys to think Aunty Annie is going mad?
p11 How do we know Aunty Annie has given Donna money before?
p13 Why does Luke stop Joe handing his phone to Annie?

Personal response
p17 Do you think Aunty Annie should tell the police?
- Do you think Donna would have got away with the crime if Luke hadn't found her out?
- Do you think Joe helped solve the mystery?

Author's style

p11 What expression does the author use when Donna says her aunty is going mad?
p15 Which speech verb does the author use to show that Annie is really angry?
p18 Why does the author use the word 'importantly' to describe how Luke is speaking?

21

Characters

- Joe
- Tracey
- Luke
- Kay

Setting the scene

Luke and Joe are kicking a football around. Kay and Tracey are sitting on the bench watching them. They start to talk about all the muggings that have been going on in the estate. Kay reckons she knows who is behind it all.

Joe: So what about all these muggings then?

Tracey: What?

Luke: You know, this guy who keeps turning up on doorsteps and mugging people.

Tracey: Oh that. Big deal. A few people had their wallets nicked. Much worse stuff goes on around here all the time.

Kay: Hey, my cousin was one of the people who had stuff nicked. And she's got a baby. Now she's scared of opening the door in case she gets mugged again.

Tracey: Oh. Sorry. It's just...

Kay: Just what?

Tracey: Well, I don't know. It's just not all that big a deal is it?

Kay: What! Some guy mugging people on their doorsteps in broad daylight, on our estate? Of course it's a big deal. What about that poor old guy?

Tracey: Who?

Joe: Yeah! The guy who got taken to hospital after he was mugged. They said he had a heart attack!

Tracey: But he was old so he might have had a heart attack anyway.

Kay: Listen, my Nan knows that guy. She said he was fine until the mugging.

Luke: *(thinking)* Someone should do something about it.

Joe: Yeah? Like what?

Luke: I don't know.

Joe: Well, you're the clever detective kid. You work it out!

Kay: You don't have to work it out. We know who it is anyway.

Luke: Really? And who is that?

Kay: That nasty piece of work Danny Morris is behind all this. We all know it.

Tracey: Well if it's that obvious why haven't the police worked it out?

Kay: Because they're stupid. It's obvious who it is but they don't get it. Either that or they're just like you Tracey, they don't think it matters.

Tracey: I said I was sorry! I do think it matters. I just wasn't thinking.

Kay: The police just don't really care about a few wallets getting nicked even if it scares us.

Luke: There is something we could do.

Joe: What's that?

Luke: We could go to the police.

Joe: Are you crazy?

Tracey: You're out of your mind!

Kay: You want to grass up Danny Morris?

Joe: Nobody from round here talks to the police. You don't do that. You know that.

Luke: And that's the problem. The police can't really do much about thugs like Danny Morris, because nobody round here wants to be seen helping the police.

Tracey: Yeah, well that's just what it's like and it isn't going to change!

Luke: But we should do something about it. It's time we all stood up to people like Danny Morris.

Joe: Yeah! I'm with you on that!

Tracey: Listen to you two – talking like crime fighting heroes!

Kay: Er, you might want to shut up guys.

Joe: Why? I'm not scared of Danny Morris.

Kay: It's just that Danny Morris is right behind you.

Joe: *(turning around)* What!

Luke:	There's nobody there.
Joe:	That's just not funny!
Kay and Tracey:	HA HA HA HA HA!

Quiz

Text comprehension

p23 Why is Kay cross that Tracey thinks the muggings are no big deal?

p27–28 Do you think telling the police can help stop crime?

p28 Why does Kay say that Danny Morris is standing behind the boys?

Vocabulary

p23 Find a word meaning 'stolen'.

p26 Find a word meaning 'clear'.

p27 Find a word meaning 'bullying criminals'.

Before reading Dumb Criminals

Find out about

- how some criminals are so stupid the police catch them easily.

New vocabulary

p32 wasting	**p35** conference
p34 witness	**p38** vandalised
p34 permanent	**p38** extinguishers

Introduction

Many criminals are caught by clever detective work, but some criminals do such stupid things that it is easy for the police to catch them. The police have described some of these criminals as the dumbest criminals ever.

Dumb Criminals

Getting Caught

Criminals do their best not to get caught by the police. But most criminals do get caught in the end. Some criminals are caught by clever detectives, some criminals are grassed up to the police by other criminals and some criminals get caught because they do something really, really stupid.

I've Got Your Number!

A man in South Africa walked into a police station. He told the police that his phone had been stolen at gunpoint. The police asked the man some questions about his phone and they wrote down his phone number. Then one of the police officers called the phone number. The phone rang... in the man's pocket! He had lied that his phone had been stolen but he hadn't even turned it off! The man was arrested for wasting police time. The police then told the media that they had caught "the dumbest criminal".

Marked Men

Two men were seen trying to break into a house.
The police were called and were given a description
of the car the men drove away in. A witness said
that the men might be wearing false beards. It
turned out that the men had drawn false beards on
their faces with a permanent marker pen. The police
found the car and the men still had the marker pen
false beards on their faces!

Whoops!

John Comparetto was at a conference. He was in the toilets when a man held him up at gunpoint. John handed over some money to the thief. But then he and some other men chased the thief and caught him. What really stupid thing had this thief done? John Comparetto was a police chief and the conference he was at was a police conference! All the other men were police officers too!

Photo Boy

A thief broke into Marc Fisher's house one night.
He found some money, a new coat and a laptop.
The thief decided to leave the Fishers something
to remember him by. He put the new coat on, held
up the money and took a photo of himself. Then
he uploaded the photo to his victim's Facebook
page. He had just handed his victim a photo of
himself at the scene of the crime! Of course, he was
caught. One police officer said, "I've seen a lot, but
this is the most stupid criminal I've ever seen."

The Sign of the Idiot

A teenager vandalised a campsite building and sprayed the building with fire extinguishers. He wrote on the wall 'Thanks for the stay'. Then he wrote his own name! Police found him by entering his name in a computer system. A police officer said, "This crime is up there with the dumbest of all in the criminal league table. There are some pretty stupid criminals around, but to leave your own name at the scene of the crime takes the biscuit."

Quiz

Text comprehension

Literal comprehension
p32 What dumb thing did this criminal do?
p35 What mistake did John Comparetto's thief make?
p38 Why did the police think this was the dumbest crime?

Inferential comprehension
p32 What could the man have done to avoid being caught out?
p36 Why might the thief have wanted to put his photo on Marc Fisher's Facebook?
p38 Why did the policeman use the expression 'takes the biscuit'?

Personal response
p35 How do you think the thief felt when he realised John Comparetto was a policeman?
- Do you think most criminals are stupid?
- What do you think the police think of dumb criminals?

Non-fiction features

p31 Why is this picture making a joke of police line-ups?
p35 Why is 'Whoops!' a good heading for this page?
p35 Why do the last two sentences on this page end with exclamation marks?

Published by Pearson Education Limited, Edinburgh Gate, Harlow, Essex, CM20 2JE.

www.pearsonschoolsandfecolleges.co.uk

Text © Pearson Education Limited 2012

Edited by Ruth Emm
Designed by Tony Richardson and Siu Hang Wong
Original illustrations © Pearson Education Limited 2012
Illustrated by Daniel Tarrant
Cover design by Siu Hang Wong
Cover illustration © Pearson Education Limited 2012

The right of Benjamin Hulme-Cross to be identified as author of this work has been asserted by
him in accordance with the Copyright, Designs and Patents Act 1988.

First published 2012

2023
16

British Library Cataloguing in Publication Data
A catalogue record for this book is available from the British Library

ISBN 978 0 435 07152 3

Printed in Great Britain by Ashford Colour Press Ltd.

Acknowledgements
The author and publisher would like to thank the following individuals and organisations for
permission to reproduce photographs:

(Key: b-bottom; c-centre; l-left; r-right; t-top)

Alamy Images: Ace Stock Limited 34t, Mark Bourdillon 37c, UpperCut Images 1, 31, 35, Vario
Images GMBH & Co. KG 33, zoonar.com 36; Pearson Education Ltd: David Sanderson 38;
Shutterstock.com: Alhovik 34c, Uss Sergey Valentinovich 32, Willee Cole 34cr

Cover images: Back: Alamy Images: Mark Bourdillon

All other images © Pearson Education

Every effort has been made to contact copyright holders of material reproduced in this book. Any
omissions will be rectified in subsequent printings if notice is given to the publishers.